Original title:
Beneath the Tropic Sun

Copyright © 2025 Creative Arts Management OÜ
All rights reserved.

Author: Gideon Barrett
ISBN HARDBACK: 978-1-80581-525-9
ISBN PAPERBACK: 978-1-80581-052-0
ISBN EBOOK: 978-1-80581-525-9

Harmonies Written in the Waves

The seagulls squawk a tune,
While crabs do the cha-cha dance.
The ocean hums a mellow tune,
As fish throw a beachside prance.

Sun hats tipped at a jaunty angle,
Sunglasses hide a sleepy glare.
A dolphin grins with a twisty dangle,
While sunscreen flies through the air.

Reflections on a Liquid Canvas

Mirrors splash with little waves,
Blue drinks spill on sandy shores.
Fishermen gather what it braves,
While sea turtles peek through doors.

A piña colada sings its song,
As flip-flops dance a jolly jig.
The beach volleyball crew tags along,
With sunscreen smeared on the big pig!

Dreams Adrift on Whispering Breezes

Kites flutter like butterflies,
As ice cream drips down on toes.
A pelican flaps as if it flies,
With fishy wishes nobody knows.

Beachcombers stroll in comical glee,
Finding shells that look like hats.
Giggling seagulls perched on a tree,
Join in the fun of silly spats.

Treasures Carried by the Tides

Crabs parade in a funky line,
Boots filled with sand, oh what a sight!
Starfish pose, sipping on brine,
Shells clinking in the morning light.

A treasure chest full of lost socks,
Is what the waves have tossed today.
Barrels of laughter, no ticking clocks,
In this whimsical land of play.

Secrets of the Tropical Breeze

A parrot squawks a silly tune,
Trying to dance by the light of the moon.
Coconuts rolling, oh what a sight,
As monkeys compete in a wild kite flight.

The sand's too hot for my little toes,
And crabs keep stealing my snacks, I suppose!
A hula girl winks with a mischievous glee,
While I try to not fall in the sea.

A Tapestry of Sunlit Shores

Seagulls argue over a lone fish bone,
While I sip my drink on a foldable throne.
The waves come crashing with a noisy cheer,
As beach balls bounce to the sound of a sneer.

Sunscreen slicks my arms like a funny glaze,
My hat blows away in the gusts of sun rays.
The lifeguard snores whilst watching the tide,
And a sandcastle leans, filled with pride!

Vibrant Hues of Island Hearts

The sunset paints the sky like a clown,
With colors so bright, it could paint a town!
Kids yell and splash in the warm, blue waves,
As sunburned tourists make goofy saves.

Flip-flops crunch on a path of warm sand,
While a piglet trots with a drink in its hand.
Tropical fruits in the mix of the fun,
A pineapple dance, oh, my heart's on the run!

Where Palms Sway in Unity

Palm trees gossip in the soft summer breeze,
While I try to catch some more z's with ease.
A crab in a tux stumbles over a shell,
As laughter erupts, oh it's ringing a bell!

The hammock sings songs of a lazy day,
While kids run wild in a bright, sunny fray.
With each silly wave that comes rushing by,
I can't help but chuckle, oh me, oh my!

Golden Dawn Over Emerald Waves

Fried eggs on sand, seagulls in flight,
The sun yawns wide, oh what a sight!
Flip-flops stuck in gooey tar,
A crab steals your lunch, that's just bizarre!

Morning coffee served in a shell,
Bubbling laugh, who can tell?
Sunglasses perched on a dog's head,
Life's a joy, when you're this well fed!

Dance of the Palm Fronds

Swinging leaves in a windy breeze,
They wave goodbye, like they're at ease!
A coconut drops, a bonk on the head,
That's what you get for not seeing red!

Grass skirts twirl, the lizards cheer,
Their moves are sharp, there's nothing to fear!
Watch out for the sand that sticks like glue,
Your flip-flop's off, but your humor's true!

Warm Embrace of the Noonday Light

Sweaty brows and a melting ice,
A sunburned nose? That's just so nice!
Sipping juice from a funky glass,
While the towel thief sneaks off with class!

Smart hats sit upon lazy jaws,
As seagulls squawk, despite the applause!
Sunblock lathered, like whipped cream spread,
Watch out for those waves, it's easier said!

Secrets of the Sapphire Sea

Splash of water, a fishy show,
Why does that swimsuit feel like a bow?
Bubbles rise in a watery dance,
A jellyfish stings? It's just a chance!

Creatures chatter in the coral maze,
Sneaky seaweed in a playful haze!
Mermaids giggle, what a strange sight,
Tickling the waves in sheer delight!

Harmony in Nature's Embrace

In the trees, a parrot sings,
Swinging hard on silly swings.
Monkeys dance with clumsy feet,
While laughing crabs just can't be beat.

A toucan slips on mango peels,
Spinning hapless, oh, how it reels!
Laughter echoes through the glade,
With every wacky, wild charade.

Sun-Drenched Dreams at Daybreak

At dawn, the roosters take the stage,
Bumbling through their morning rage.
The sunbeams tickle sleepy eyes,
While squirrels plot their next surprise.

A lizard laughs in sun's embrace,
As it slides down, a clumsy race.
Coffee brews, a fragrant cheer,
As island life kicks into gear.

Whispers of Paradise in the Wind

Palm fronds sway like a silly dance,
The wind lifts skirts, oh what a chance!
Coconuts drop with a thud so loud,
As beachgoers scramble in a crowd.

A crab sprints sideways, full of glee,
While seagulls squawk, plotting a spree.
In this land of giggles and fun,
Nature chuckles under the sun.

Flavors Purged with the Fresh Ocean Air

Fish tacos fly like summer kites,
Surfboards wipe out in wild fights.
Limes and salsa, a zesty twist,
While seagulls eye a tourist's wrist.

The winds blow in a fragrant tease,
As sunburnt folks nibble with ease.
With every bite, the laughter grows,
A feast of fun, where no one knows.

Embrace of the Equatorial Sun

A penguin in shorts found his way,
He danced on the beach, come what may.
With sunscreen smeared on his beak,
He chirped at the sun, feeling quite sleek.

A cactus wore shades, looking quite cool,
While lizards played chess by the pool.
They chuckled and joked with each sunny ray,
In a realm where the funny just loves to play.

Journeys Across the Sun-Drenched Sands

A crab in a bucket listed his plans,
To build a small castle with his own hands.
Seagulls all cawed, what a sight!
As the sun overhead turned everything bright.

A dolphin sported a bowler hat,
While a beach ball rolled, oh what a spat!
Sandcastles crumbled like dreams gone awry,
Yet laughter echoed beneath the clear sky.

Starlit Conversations by the Shore

Nights by the water, a clam sings a tune,
With a starfish dancer who sways by the moon.
They share silly stories 'bout life 'neath the tide,
As crabs in tuxedos all come to the side.

A fish in a coat picks up a drink,
While plankton ponder what they can think.
Whispers of laughter drift out to the sea,
In a world where the funny swims wild and free.

Memories Lounging in Dappled Sunlight

A monkey in shades feels oh-so-fine,
Nibbling on coconuts while sipping on brine.
The best of the jokes always come from the trees,
With parrots that echo, "More mangoes, please!"

A turtle in flip-flops, slow but so spry,
Caught up in the antics of the bright sky.
Memories swirl like leaves in a breeze,
With giggles resounding amongst the tall trees.

Enchantment in Sunbeams and Waves

Sunbeams dance on bubbling waves,
Fish in shades do antics brave.
A crab with shades, a starfish snorts,
In laughter, our joy never supports.

Flip-flops flying, hats take flight,
Chasing dreams in sheer delight.
A seagull steals a sandwich quick,
While beach balls bounce like magic tricks.

Tales of Shadows and Light's Embrace

In the light, shadows play their tricks,
A coconut drops, oh what a mix!
We chase the laughs, the sunburns too,
With every slip, we find our cue.

Sandy toes and silly hats,
Our sunscreen's gone, oh where's the pats?
A lizard laughs, or so it seems,
As we dive into our sun-kissed dreams.

Mermains and Mystic Sands

Mermains wiggle, tales to tell,
Their laughter echoes like a bell.
With seaweed wigs, they dance and sway,
Inviting us to join their play.

A buried treasure made of schnoz,
Turns out to be a crab's great cause.
With laughter bubbling, crabs parade,
In this sandy, wavy charade.

The Flavor of a Tropical Evening

Coconuts toast to twilight's art,
While pineapples play a juicy part.
A parrot squawks a tune so sweet,
As we dance to the rhythm of our feet.

Swaying palm trees gossip low,
As twinkling lights start to glow.
With laughter in the evening air,
Every sip is a giggle, fair and rare.

Dreams Woven in Warmth

Sandy toes and sunburn's grace,
Ice cream drips, a sticky race.
Flip flops squeak, they dance along,
To the beat of a beachy song.

Coconuts wear silly hats,
Crabs scuttle, like mini brats.
Palm trees sway, they shimmy slow,
While sunburnt tourists put on a show.

Echoing Laughter Amongst the Flora

Buzzing bees play hide and seek,
While geckos giggle, so to speak.
Flowers bloom in colors loud,
Making even cacti feel proud.

Monkeys throw their jokes from trees,
While parrots laugh, 'Oh, please, please!'
Life's a joke in colors bright,
As we dance through day and night.

Mirage of the Endless Summer

Sips of coconut, sweet delight,
In the sun, all feels just right.
Chasing waves with laughter clear,
While sun hats fly, oh dear, oh dear!

Surfers tumble, splash and play,
As jellyfish join in the fray.
An endless scene of joyful glee,
Where even the sun rolls with esprit.

Solstice of the Sweetened Air

Fruit stands stacked like mighty towers,
Giggling kids run wild for hours.
The sun glows bright, a bold buffoon,
As the ice cream truck honks its tune.

Lizards stretch in sun's warm kiss,
While tourists chase the perfect bliss.
A festival of smiles and cheer,
Where laughter lingers, always near.

In the Shade of the Mango Tree

Sitting here, my hat's gone rogue,
A mango dropped and hit my bogue.
The squirrels plan a sneaky heist,
While I just dream of mango ice.

Their chatter fills the afternoon,
I laugh and wish to sing a tune.
But with the fruit flies in my hair,
I think I'll just stay right in there.

Oh, life is ripe and full of cheer,
As long as snacks are always near.
I'll watch the world while sipping tea,
In my shady spot; just me and me!

Glimmers Found in Hidden Cove

There's treasure in a shell I found,
But it's a jellybean I crowned.
I told the seagulls of my quest,
They laughed and left me quite distressed.

The waves roll in with such a tease,
As crabs scuttle by with the breeze.
"Come dance with me!" I say in jest,
But they just scuff their tiny chest.

With every splash, my troubles fade,
The sea is bright, I'm not afraid.
In this cove, my heart takes flight,
Hidden things sparkle in the light.

Dances with Fiery Sunsets

The sun decides to do a jig,
While palm trees sway and rocks look big.
I join the dance with flailing arms,
As evening's hues work all their charms.

A piña colada's on my mind,
But I drop it? Oh, how unkind!
The dance goes on, I waddle free,
Who needs a drink? Just look at me!

Each cloud's a partner, pink and road
Adventures lie in sunset's code.
I'll dance until my feet can't stand,
And then I'll fall upon the sand.

Rhythm of the Salty Sea

The ocean hums a silly tune,
As me and fish now share a room.
I flap around, I won't be shy,
Think I'm a mermaid? Give it a try!

A starfish laughs and rolls with glee,
While jellyfish float like they're on spree.
Is that a dolphin doing a dive?
Or just my buddy trying to thrive?

The salty spray is quite the blast,
I ride the waves and hope they last.
With every splash, my laughter flows,
For under waves, anything goes!

Luminescence of Sunset Bliss

As day drifts down, colors play,
Crabs in concert start their ballet.
Flip-flops slapping, laughter flies,
While penguins dance under painted skies.

A beach ball bounces, dogs on a spree,
Surfboards wobble, oh what a sight to see!
Coconut drinks in sunlit cheer,
Splashing water, polar bears near!

Seagulls squawk, trying to chat,
While tourists argue over a hat.
Flip a hot dog, watch it fly,
Next to a turtle wearing a tie.

Sandcastles rise, then quickly fall,
A kid's great plan gets no recall.
Laughter bubbles, waves crash in,
Golden moments, let the fun begin!

Radiance in the Heart of Paradise

A parrot shrieks, and then takes flight,
Hiding from sunbeams, what a sight!
The hammock sways, a nap on hold,
With ice cream dribbling, stories told.

Palm trees sway like dancers free,
Flipping drinks like circus feats.
Sunburnt noses, red and bright,
In coconut shells, we find delight.

Sun hats on, with smiles so wide,
The beach is our merry ride.
Jellyfish jiggle, crabs take a bow,
Who knew nature could be so wow?

Sunglasses on, we fake a tan,
While sunscreen's a battle, oh what a plan!
Day fades slowly, laughter remains,
With tales of the ocean in our veins.

Haikus in the Shade of Palms

Seagulls swoop and dive,
Chips disappear in thin air,
Fried joy on the breeze.

Coconut surprises,
Every sip's a giggle spree,
Laughter in the shade.

Sunburns and sun hats,
Sandy toes and ice cream joys,
Life is best with laughs.

Underneath the palms,
Nap or dance, no rules apply,
Fun is our only guide!

The Dance of Colorful Skippers

Butterflies frolic, colors bright,
A dance-off under the afternoon light.
Sipping lemonade, bees conspire,
While ants march like soldiers, never tire.

Jelly's for jumping, waves for surfing,
The ocean's a stage, nature's perfect casting.
With each gust of wind, hats fly away,
Tilting sideways in the warm sun's sway.

Friends play frisbee, dodging the pines,
Frogs leap along to their favorite lines.
A crab in a tutu steals the show,
As giggles rise where the cool breezes blow.

Even the sun has a grin today,
Casting shadows that dance and sway.
With memories painted in colors bold,
The warmth of laughter never grows old.

Songs of the Coral-tinged Waves

Jellyfish dancing, they wiggle in glee,
A crab with a top hat sips coconut tea.
Gull and pelican in a sing-off so grand,
While fish steal the spotlight, just as they planned.

Octopus plays the drums with no fuss,
Sea turtles grooving, oh what a plus!
A conch acts as a trumpet, loud and clear,
While starfish cheer on, with a round of good cheer.

The Rhythm of Radiant Days

Sunshine splashes, like paint on a wall,
Cockatoos chatter; who's having a ball?
Lizards in sunglasses are taking the stage,
While bees bumble dance, buzzing off-page.

Coconuts rolling, a hilarious race,
A parrot mocks, while we giggle in place.
The heat makes us melt like ice cream in hand,
Still everyone laughs; we're a merry band.

Tropical Serenade Under the Stars

Fireflies flicker like notes in the night,
Geckos are crooning, what a funny sight!
A ukulele strums along with the breeze,
As banter erupts like giggles from trees.

The moon grins wide, a curious chap,
While sloths sway slowly, caught in a nap.
With laughter in the air and joy all around,
It's a party of creatures, no frowns to be found.

Embracing the Lush Green Canopy

Monkeys are swinging, inventing new games,
While frogs play charades, calling out names.
Parrots are gossiping, colorfully loud,
As turtles roll by, feeling smug and proud.

The vines are a dance floor for bugs overhead,
With beetles tap-dancing instead of in bed.
Each leaf is a stage for a comedy show,
In this jungle of fun, laughter continues to flow.

Fables of the Sunlit Oasis

In a land where cacti wear hats,
Lizards dance with chattering rats.
A parrot sings a silly tune,
While sipping lemonade with a raccoon.

Every sip's a burst of cheer,
As bees buzz by with tales to hear.
A cactus croaks, 'I need some sunscreen!'
The sun shines bright, a giggling machine.

They tell of a frog with a great big grin,
Who lost his shades while doing a spin.
Fables woven of laughter and light,
In the oasis, the world feels just right.

So come and share a whimsical tale,
With laughter echoing on the breeze's trail.
In this sunlit gem, no gloom resides,
Just silly stories where joy abides.

Unfurling Petals in the Heat

In gardens where flowers giggle and sway,
Petals yawn at the start of the day.
A sunflower wearing shades so bright,
Tells jokes to the roses, what a sight!

A butterfly asks, 'What's your best stance?'
The daisies reply, 'We just love to dance!'
They twirl and spin in the warm sunbeam,
While the gardener snickers, or so it seems.

Tulips gossip while sipping sweet tea,
'Have you heard what the weeds said about me?'
With laughter that pulls at the vine,
Every bloom feels happy and fine.

So here's to petals in the summer blaze,
Unfurling cheekily, lost in a daze.
In the floral cabaret, all's a show,
Colorful capers that constantly grow.

Stargazers of the Summer Night

As the sun dips low, the stars come out,
Crickets chirp, there's no doubt.
A raccoon holds a chart with great pride,
'Look, a star shaped like a slice of pie!'

Owls wink as they plan their spree,
While fireflies twist in jubilee.
A chipmunk leaps, bumps into a tree,
'Excuse me, stargazing's fun for me!'

They declare a contest of who can find,
The funniest shapes that come to mind.
The night is filled with giggles and sighs,
As constellations paint the skies.

So if you wander where the wild things play,
Join the jesters beneath the Milky Way.
For laughter echoes, in ample degree,
In a nocturnal dance, wild and free.

Laughter in the Leaves Above

The trees are swaying with leafy glee,
As squirrels leap from branch to tree.
A monkey swings with a cheeky grin,
Saying, 'My friends, let the fun begin!'

Acorns drop like silly rain,
And the birds chat 'bout their latest gain.
'Did you see that twig? What a blast!'
Echoes of joy in nature's cast.

Leaves rustle with whispers and gaffes,
As the wind tells jokes, eliciting laughs.
A wise old owl rolls his eyes in style,
While a young bud chuckles all the while.

So when you wander through nature's embrace,
Listen closely for the laughter's trace.
In the canopy high, where friends unite,
Joyous echoes dance in the soft moonlight.

Treasures in the Coral Depths

Diving down where fish conspire,
I found a shoe instead of a lyre.
Sea cucumbers dance like they care,
But all they do is just sit there.

A goldfish laughing with delight,
Waves of giggles, what a sight!
Coral castles, bright and wild,
Building dreams just like a child.

Giant clams attempt to sing,
Yet all they do is flap and cling.
A treasure chest with rusty key,
Holding nothing, just a seaweed spree.

So come and join this raucous spree,
Where fish wear hats and sing with glee.
Life's too short to take a dip,
Without a laugh or quirky quip!

Echoes of the Island Heart

On the shore, the waves do kerplunk,
While seagulls dance, heads like a junk.
There's a crab that wears my flip-flop,
Snapping at tourists, can't make it stop!

A coconut rolls, it's quite the tease,
Rolling away with the ocean breeze.
It found a friend, a jellyfish,
Wiggling, waggling, makes quite a dish!

The parrots squawk in a loud debate,
Arguing if it's wise to wait.
Or why the sun could be so hot,
When it's really just a giant pot!

Laughter echoes through the sandy lane,
With dancing feet, we'll never complain.
Life's a feast, grab a fork and spoon,
Let's dig into this island tune!

Serenity in a Tropical Haven

In a hammock swaying near the bay,
I saw a cat who thought he could play.
Chasing lizards, making a fuss,
His tail a rocket; oh, what a rush!

Palm trees wave in a silly dance,
While tourists try to find romance.
But all they find is sand in shoes,
And the sunburn that they didn't choose!

A monkey swings with such great flair,
Stealing snacks without a care.
While locals grin at the scene above,
Nature's laughter, a tale of love.

So join the fun in this breezy spot,
With mischief mixed in every plot.
Serenity is just a laugh away,
In this tropical wonder, come what may!

The Taste of Salt and Sunshine

Sipping drinks that look like art,
With umbrellas that fall apart.
A taste of salt, a splash of cheer,
Mixing sunshine with frosty beer!

Fish tacos sing with joy and zest,
Each crisp bite, they are the best.
While coconuts roll just for fun,
They're plotting mischief in the sun!

A conch shell tried to tell a joke,
But all it did was make us choke.
Salt in the air, and laughter loud,
Island life draws a bustling crowd.

Come savor this salty-laden feast,
Where laughter floats, at least, at least!
Each bite a giggle, each sip a cheer,
In this sweet land, we hold dear!

Whispers of the Golden Horizon

In a hammock, I swayed and grinned,
My cat stole my drink, now he's pinned.
The fruit flies buzz, they lead the show,
Mangoes take flight, just watch them go!

Tanned tourists aim to pose all day,
While I dodge sunscreen like it's a plague.
Flip-flops flop as they try to strut,
But pegged by a wave, they slip and cut!

Seagulls squawk with a cheeky flair,
Snatching lunches from folks unaware.
"Hey, my sandwich!" a beachgoer yells,
While I savor snacks as the chaos swells!

Sunburns try to pass as fashion's flair,
With patterns red, like peppery stare.
But laughter erupts as the sunsets sink,
In funny moments, life's sweetly pink!

Shadows Dance on Warm Sands

Footprints mingle, then quickly fade,
Like reasoning after a mojito shade.
An umbrella flips in a comical twist,
My beachside ballet got lost in the mist!

Tanned bodies dance, though they can't quite groove,
Falling like waves that can't find their move.
Sunhats fly off, in gusts of delight,
As laughter and giggles take full flight!

Children's sandcastles, all towers of dreams,
Get washed away by the surf's silly schemes.
"Mother, it's gone!" the little one cries,
As a wave lingers with comedic goodbyes!

A crab decides it's his time to shine,
Strutting sideways, thinking he's fine.
All the while, I chuckle and cheer,
Because in this dance, joy's always near!

The Lure of Coastal Dreams

On sandy shores, my flip-flops cried,
As I raced with the seagulls side by side.
An ice cream cone, teetering on high,
Melted away, oh my, oh my!

Hot sun above, I'm a melting treat,
While chasing crabs that dance on their feet.
They scoot away with a cheeky snicker,
Like they're the sassy ones, oh what a kicker!

Beach games start, but chaos takes hold,
With frisbees lost and laughter bold.
"Is that your balloon?" I inquire with glee,
While the tide swells, setting all balloons free!

And as shells wink, secrets they keep,
I shrug and sink into a nap so deep.
For coastal dreams are not born of sleep,
But of laughter and love—a treasure to reap!

Echoes of Sunlit Embrace

In the warmth, we bask like lazy lizards,
Swapping stories and impromptu quiz-ards.
"Who wore it best?" the gossip runs wild,
As someone spots a beach bum child!

Sun hats bob like boats at sea,
While sunscreen battles that scream with glee.
All the while, someone's cellphone blares,
An unexpected remix that captures stares!

The tide rolls in with a glimmering laugh,
Carrying shells and a history graph.
We chase the waves with a daring yell,
Digging for treasures where laughter fell!

As the sun dips low, we sing our songs,
Of sandy toes and love that prolongs.
In echoes bright, our memories twirl,
Wrapped in joy—a whimsical whirl!

Reflections on a Silvered Bay

In the bay, a fish sings high,
Wearing a hat as it flops by.
Sunburnt legs and splashes loud,
Chasing crabs, I feel quite proud.

A turtle waves with reckless sass,
While seagulls giggle, trying to pass.
My ice cream melts in the hot air,
Scoop on my nose, a sticky affair.

The boat rocked gently, then gave a squeak,
I startled a catfish, oh, what a peek!
The sun winks down, spiking the fun,
Life's a splash when you're on the run.

A floatie whale begins to dance,
While I'm stuck in a beach chair trance.
With laughter ringing, we soak it all,
Don't mind the seagulls, they just squall.

Memories Carved in Sunlit Stone

In sandy pits, with toes all jammed,
We sculpted castles, a plan so grand.
But tides crept in with a giggling roar,
Our kingdom fell—now sandy lore.

The sun is bright, my hat flies away,
Chasing it down, I'm in a play.
A crab on the run, clinks his shell,
While I stumble, tripping, oh well!

Flops and giggles, my friends do boast,
While I dive in, a splash and a toast.
We toast to the sun, bright and bold,
Memories sticky as ice cream cold.

Little sunburns make life a jest,
With laughter shared, I feel so blessed.
We dance and sing, till daylight's end,
With tales of crabs, our sandy friends.

Whispers of the Southern Breeze

A breeze comes in, it carries tales,
Of flamingos in absurd veil trails.
They strut with flair, like old-time stars,
Wiggling their wings, oh, what bizarre!

The sun spins low, a golden disk,
While sandcastles don masks of risk.
My friend slipped down, a graceless slide,
Laughter erupted from topside tide.

In the shade, I sip my sweet drink,
While fish plot out their next big wink.
We giggle as shadows start to creep,
Ticklish toes in the water, they leap.

Whispers float by, the breeze is playing,
With salty jokes that keeps us swaying.
Life's but a dance, caught in the swirl,
Amongst the tides, let laughter unfurl.

Sunlit Shadows on the Shore

On the shore, shadows play leapfrog,
While I chase down a drifting log.
My friends building pyramids of sand,
Look up to see their towers stand.

A crab in a hat rolls past my knee,
Trying to join our jubilee.
With sandals flung, my toes dig deep,
I rock the boat—oh, what a leap!

The frisbee twirls, half-goes awry,
While I dive down with a little cry.
The waves all giggle, splashing too,
As sun-kissed hearts dance into the blue.

Shells whisper secrets of days gone by,
As gulls above plot their next sly lie.
With sunlit shadows soft on the floor,
We'll giggle together, forever more.

Among the Echoes of Sandy Trails

Footprints in the sand do dance,
Crabs join in a merry prance.
Sunscreen's slathered, what a sight,
Is that a flip-flop? Oh, what a plight!

Seagulls squawk with cheeky glee,
Diving down for snacks, you see.
My sandwich flies, the ocean swells,
A feast for birds, oh, what the hells!

Kids build castles, tall and proud,
Waves wash them down like a shroud.
Yet laughter echoes, high and free,
As parents sigh, 'Just let it be!'

Chasing shadows, lost in fun,
We forget the day's almost done.
With sandy toes and salty hair,
We wave goodbye to evening air!

The Brush of Sun against Bare Skin

A sunburn's kiss on my bright nose,
Makes me look like a clown, who knows?
Sunglasses perched, I'm feeling grand,
 Until I trip on hot, soft sand!

Lemonade spills, oh what a mess,
Sticky hands in summer's dress.
Ice cream melts, drips down my chin,
Who knew such fun could come from sin?

Beach balls bounce, hitting the sand,
In a game of catch, it's unplanned.
I duck and weave but here comes a wave,
Splashing my friends, oh, how I rave!

Golden rays make shadows lurk,
Dancing 'round as parades perk.
Laughter rising as day departs,
Who knew the beach could steal our hearts?

Woven Paths Through Vibrant Flora

Through tangled vines, we take a stroll,
With bugs as pets, they steal the role.
A flower here, a flower there,
Watch out! That one bites, beware!

Butterflies flutter, what a sight,
One lands on my snack, and it takes flight.
I swipe it back, oh what a game,
Suddenly, I'm feeling lame!

Chasing shadows of palms so tall,
We bump into each other, fall.
With giggles shared, we brush off dirt,
Who knew exploring could involve flirt?

A hidden pool with sparkling sheen,
Echoes of laughter fill the green.
This jungle trip, quite the charade,
But oh what fun in leafy shade!

Buoyant Spirits in Salty Air

Up in the air, kites soar and spin,
On a windy day, let the fun begin.
A flip, a flop, and a cartwheel too,
Who knew the breeze could make me woo?

Sandy hair and salty lips,
Life's a joy ride, take some trips.
Jumping waves, trying not to fall,
Splashing water, I hear the call!

Umbrellas sway, a bright parade,
The sun gives gifts, a warm cascade.
With beach towels and laughter loud,
We're the craziest, beach-time crowd!

As evening falls with skies ablaze,
We dance like mermaids in ocean's gaze.
With buoyant spirits and hearts so light,
Who cares for troubles in this delight?

Garden of the Sunlit Realm

In a garden where cacti wear hats,
And rabbits sing songs about chitchat,
The daisies do dance, oh what a sight,
While butterflies argue who's flower's right.

A squirrel named Dave thinks he's a chef,
With acorn soufflés, quite full of zest,
But when he's done, oh what chaos reigns,
Flour all over, and chocolate stains!

The sun giggles down, with a bright golden grin,
As chickens take selfies, let the fun begin,
In this realm where laughter and sunshine blend,
Every corner alive, joy on the mend.

So come take a stroll on this funky path,
Where laughter grows wild, and happiness hath,
For in this garden, with glee all around,
The silliest creatures dance on the ground.

Radiant Visions of the Coast

By the shore where the seagulls wear shades,
And crabs think they're stars on parades,
The waves laugh loudly, tickling the sand,
While surfers attempt tricks that never go as planned.

A pelican named Pete yells, "Can I dive?"
While dolphins tease, "Come on, take a ride!"
The sun throws a party, a beachy affair,
With coconuts dancing, turned up in the air.

Sandy toes wiggle in a curious dance,
As beach balls roll by, oh what a chance,
To catch all the giggles and cheer of the tide,
As friends make a mess, filled with joy and pride.

So grab a good joke, and join in the fun,
At this coastal fiesta, oh what a run,
With the waves and the wind, laughter will soar,
In visions so radiant, you'll ask for more.

Chasing Shadows at Flowing Tides

Oh, the shadows play games at the brim of the sea,
Where pirates pretend to sip coconut tea,
With laughter and giggles, they sail and they sway,
As the tides pull and push, in a silly ballet.

A crab with a treasure, bless his little claws,
Finds shiny old buttons and a taco that was,
With a wink and a nudge, he shouts, "What a steal!"
Near the old shipwreck, oh, what a meal!

The sun takes a nap, wearing shades like a boss,
While seaweed forms wigs on a dolphin named Ross,
As the shadows grow long, oh what joyous sights,
With flip-flops and beach balls, the fun ignites.

So wander alongside the playful and spry,
At the shores where the laughter will never say die,
For chasing those shadows, oh what a delight,
Underneath laughter, everything feels right.

Harmony in the Canopy's Embrace

In the jungle, a monkey named Lou plays the drums,
While parrots throw parties, singing sweet hums,
The trees giggle softly, swaying as they sing,
In harmony bright, like a playful spring.

A sloth in a hammock is dozing away,
While raccoons throw acorns, making a display,
With giggles and wiggles, the trees hold their breath,
As vines whip and twirl in a dance—what a mess!

Sunbeams peek through, like children at play,
Saying, "Join in the fun, don't you run away!"
With critters conspiring, in this merry grove,
Each branch holds a secret, laughter's the trove.

So grab a banana, join the jubilant throng,
As the canopy hums out its jubilant song,
For harmony lives where the critters embrace,
In a world full of joy, and boundless fun's race.

The Rhythm of Rainforest Whispers

The parrots squawk, they steal my snack,
A monkey swings with a cheeky knack.
Frogs wear hats, so bright and bold,
In this green theater, the stories unfold.

Lizards dance on branches high,
While iguanas wink with a sly eye.
Rain drops down like a playful tease,
Nature laughs in the rustling leaves.

The hummingbird zooms, a tiny blur,
Chasing butterflies, causing a stir.
Mushrooms giggle in layers so neat,
Step on the wrong one, you'll admit defeat!

So come on down to this zany land,
Where creatures scramble, both weird and grand.
Every corner holds a wacky surprise,
In this wild paradise, joy never dies!

Secrets of the Sun-Kissed Isle

On a beach where sand is never still,
Turtles race down, with a curious thrill.
Coconuts tumble, rolling away,
Palm trees giggle, come join the play!

Crabs wear tuxedos, strut with flair,
While the seagulls argue without a care.
The sun dips low, a sticky sweet hue,
Even the waves join in laughing too.

Bamboo huts sway, a party inside,
Drinks are clinking, come take a ride!
Laughter bubbles like the soda pop,
When you're here, oh, you just can't stop!

At night the stars join in the jest,
Winking down at this tropical fest.
Come share a secret, a giggle or jest,
On this sun-kissed isle, you'll find the best!

Vibrant Colors of a Dreaming Tropics

Flowers in stripes, like a crazy quilt,
Dancing in patterns, with colors built.
Bees wear goggles, buzzing about,
While butterflies whisper secrets, no doubt.

The sunset splashes, a painter's delight,
As iguanas play peek-a-boo with the night.
Parrots turn heads, a fashion parade,
Who knew the jungle could be so flambé?

The river tickles as it flows with glee,
Leaves twist and turn in elaborate spree.
A pink flamingo starts to groove,
Just wait 'til you see it bust a move!

In every corner, the laughter ignites,
With chattering critters and silly sights.
Colorful dreams in this wild abode,
In the land of wonder, let joy explode!

Serenade of the Tropical Nights

Night falls softly with a twinkling shout,
As critters gather, joining the clout.
Fireflies light up in a wild ballet,
The frogs croak tunes that lead the way.

A raccoon winks with a mischievous grin,
Sharing stories of all his wins.
The stars above, they giggle and stare,
At the bashful moon, caught in its glare.

Drums beat loudly, a party so bright,
As crickets chirp, dancing in flight.
The shadows play games, just out of sight,
Spooky, cheeky, in the tropical night.

Everyone's welcome, let laughter abound,
In this wacky jungle, joy can be found.
Under the canopy, so lush and wide,
Join the serenade, let your heart glide!

Elysium of the Endless Summer

A coconut falls, it's ripe and round,
I dodge it quick, oh what a sound!
The sun is bright, my skin's a glow,
But watch out, friend, for flying mangoes in tow!

Flip-flops squeak on sandy floors,
Seagulls laugh like they've seen it before.
I wave to fish with a silly grin,
While crabs wander by, like they're in a spin!

Ice cream melts, drips down my chin,
I guess today, the ocean will win.
A mermaid giggles from the sea's embrace,
As I belly flop in a clumsy race!

Palm trees sway in rhythm and rhyme,
Every day here is summer time.
My worries fade like sand in the tide,
In this endless joy, I just can't hide!

The Print of Barefoot Adventures

Barefoot I roam, on paths of gold,
My toes in mud, a sight to behold.
I trip on a shell and let out a shout,
Guess I'll add 'surfing' to my clumsy route!

With a grass skirt on, I dance like a fool,
The locals all cheer, is it me or the two?
I spin and I twirl, my hat flies away,
The wind takes it south, where I wish I could stay!

Sipping coconuts, feeling so grand,
But watch your drink; it's a slippery hand.
A monkey swings by, it's quite a scene,
I think that's my drink? Oh, what a mean!

Beach games commence with laughter abound,
Prizes include seashells stuck in the ground.
We dig and we dive, with spirit so bright,
Life's one big giggle, from morning to night!

Colorful Echoes of Island Life

Colors pop like a painter's delight,
As I trip on a fish, it gives me a fright.
With leis around necks, we laugh and we sing,
While my ukulele's strumming, what joy it will bring!

The local cats pose with such grand flair,
They strut with pride, like they own the square.
I try their dance, but they look so confused,
Am I grooving or merely bemused?

Shells and treasures, a pirate's dream,
But half of them smell more like old ice cream.
The tide rolls in with stories to share,
As I kick up sand in a very odd air!

The sunset brings colors, a painter's embrace,
I trip on a rock, but I'm keeping my grace.
With laughter and joy, the island does sing,
In this whimsical life, I'm the merriest thing!

Beneath the Canopy of Time

The jungle hums with a curious tune,
While I stumble and fumble under the moon.
Banana peels slip like a slapstick show,
As I wave at a toucan, "Hey, what's the go?"

Frogs croak chorus, a nighttime delight,
But the bats above give me quite the fright.
I dodge a vine like a game of tag,
While a parrot caws, "You're a silly rag!"

In the midst of the trees, a hammock does sway,
But I miss the landing, oh what a display!
I crash in the leaves with a giggle so loud,
While the forest critters form a curious crowd!

As shadows dance in the fading light,
The stars peek down, what a magical sight.
With laughter and tales, under starlit rhyme,
I cherish the moments that slip through time!

Alternating Currents of Tender Calm

In the shade, a lizard grins,
As he eyes my sandwich, it begins.
I wave my hand; he darts away,
He knows not to stay for the fray.

The hammock swings with sleepy glee,
As I sip my drink and spill some tea.
A coconut drops with a funny thud,
I laugh aloud, it's just my luck!

The waves crash softly, a rhythmic dance,
The seagull steals my chips at a glance.
In this lull, there's nothing to dread,
Except for the sunburn on my head!

Flip-flops flop as I try to run,
Chasing a crab that's having too much fun.
A splash from a friend, and I take a dive,
At least in this chaos, I feel alive!

Radiance of Dappled Light

A shadow leaps, and I must flee,
The piñata swings; is it after me?
The candy bursts, and chaos reigns,
As kids dive in for their sweet gains.

The sun peeks through a leafy green,
To find my hat where the ground's unseen.
A squirrel scampers, a cheeky little chap,
Taking my lunch while I take a nap.

Laughter rings as I spill my drink,
A surprise shower, quicker than you think.
Tropical winds send my dreams adrift,
Oh, how this moment is a funny gift!

Sunlight dances on a glimmering tide,
As I attempt to surf, not much to ride.
A tumble and splash, I flop like a fish,
Well, at least it's not the wave I wished!

The Sun-Kissed Oasis of Memory

A beach ball bounces, and so do I,
Trying to catch it, much to my chagrin nearby.
The wind snickers and swats it away,
I tumble to sand, what a sunny day!

A tourist winks, "Is this your best shot?"
I shrug, while pretending it's all I've got.
Waves crash in laughter, they know the score,
I grin wide, my face locked in folklore.

Flip-flops squeak, a comic parade,
Each step a giggle, this bliss won't fade.
I wave to a crab that's digging a hole,
He pauses, curious, then rolls on a stroll.

The sun dips down, the colors ignite,
In this wild dance, it all feels just right.
We laugh at the footprints that lead to nowhere,
In this sun-kissed wonder, we savor the air!

Caress of the Gentle Trade Winds

The wind tousles hair like a playful friend,
As I chase after petals that float and bend.
They swirl around, oh what a sight,
I'm a dancing leaf in this breezy flight.

My drink is cold, but my hand is warm,
As I sip and laugh at the tiny storm.
The ice clinks, like music in a glass,
Each sip a giggle, a moment that'll pass.

A parrot squawks a ridiculous joke,
"Why did the fish bring a notebook?"
We all burst out in a fit of glee,
It's the kind of humor that echoes at sea.

The sun sets low, painting skies so bright,
As we share our tales, our hearts feel light.
With the wind in our sails, we sail on fun,
This adventure shared, we've only begun!

The Laughter of Tropical Skies

A parrot told a joke so bright,
It made the palm trees lean with delight.
Monkeys giggled in the warm, warm air,
As coconuts dropped without a care.

The sun, a big clown in yellow and gold,
Paints the world in stories untold.
Flip-flops slap as kids run around,
Chasing waves and laughter, what a sound!

The beach huts sway, with laughter they dance,
Shells whisper secrets, given the chance.
A crab in a top hat tried to impress,
But slipped on a banana peel, causing a mess!

Here the sun wears shades, just for fun,
While sipping lemonade, oh what a run!
With every splash, life bursts into cheer,
Under skies that sparkle, far and near.

Where Ocean Meets the Horizon

A whale sang tunes that made waves giggle,
While dolphins danced, oh what a wiggle!
Seagulls played cards with the biggest catch,
While fishermen shouted, 'What a match!'

The sun dipped low, like a sleepy old man,
Painting the sky, oh what a plan!
Kids with buckets chased fish with glee,
While the tide chuckled, 'Come play with me!'

Sand castles grew, as stubborn as cows,
Until waves crashed in, with mighty 'howls!'
A pirate parrot squawked, 'Where's me gold?'
But found only flip-flops, old and bold.

And as the sun set, colors all tangled,
Fish told stories, so funny and dangled.
Under a sky that yawned and stretched,
The ocean chuckled, no secrets fetched.

Legends of the Lush Canopy

A sloth once claimed he could jump high,
But nap-time won, much to his sigh.
Parrots wore hats, fancied up bright,
Debating the fashion of day and night.

In this jungle, a monkey ran fast,
Chasing the rumors of a fun-filled blast.
While turtles laughed, 'We'll get there slow!'
Giggling softly, 'We took the wrong road!'

Trees whispered jokes in the rustling breeze,
"Why did the coconut refuse to freeze?"
Because it found out the ice was too chill,
And would rather hang out with the freest of thrill!

With fruits having parties, a banana parade,
Each swing and giggle, a memory made.
In a canopy bustling and oh so lush,
Every rustle and laugh made hearts positively blush.

Mirage of Distant Horizons

A mirage danced with a curious grin,
While camels tried hard not to fall in.
The horizon teased with a wink and a joke,
"Is it water or just smoke?"

Sandy feasts of laughter filled the air,
With sandcastles wobbling without a care.
A cactus played tag with an unseen friend,
While tumbleweeds rolled, just around the bend.

The sun, a jester in a big, floppy hat,
Cackled aloud at a sunbaked cat.
"Why don't you fetch?" it loudly quipped,
As the cat squinted, slowly tipped.

Dunes shimmered gold, with giggles that rose,
Every breeze carried humor; oh, how it flows!
In a land so bright where dreams take flight,
The mirage plays games, from day into night.

Festivities Under the Flaming Sky

Dancing under palm tree hats,
Sipping drinks from coconuts,
Everyone laughs at clumsy gaffes,
While dogs chase crabs in funny ruts.

Late-night feasts on sandy shores,
Grilling fish with shaky hands,
Locals joke of ancient scores,
As laughter travels in giggled bands.

Flip-flops flapping, a wild dance,
Twisting bodies in bright attire,
Even the sun starts to prance,
As if competing for laughter's choir.

When the stars peek out with glee,
Making wishes seem so grand,
We trip over our own feet,
Celebrating this magic land.

Basking in the Glow of the Tropics

Sunscreen battles clogging pores,
Sticky laughter fills the air,
Tanned folks tumble through the stores,
As cashier grins with ocean flair.

Ice-cream melts in the hot sun,
Drips down knees, a sticky fight,
A child squeals, "Can we just run?"
As the waves claim our delight.

Beach games spark the silly war,
With sand castles meeting doom,
A frisbee flies, oh, what a score,
While gulls gossip from their plume.

Chasing shadows, we all glide,
Spinning tales of the day's thrill,
In this glow, we laugh and bide,
Savoring life, our hearts fulfill.

Lost in the Warmth of Island Time

Silly clocks don't stand a chance,
Time meanders like a stream,
Napping under bright sun's dance,
Dreams mingle with ice-cream.

Outrigger sails on dodgy seas,
While fishermen laugh over tea,
Hoping for bites, oh, please,
Instead catch seaweed, what a spree!

Sunburnt noses, a comic sight,
Friends pointing, teasing with flair,
"Who needs shirts, when you feel right?"
As sand gets everywhere, oh dear!

Evenings blend with fiery tales,
Jokes wash up just like the tide,
Underneath the starry trails,
We find joy in every ride.

The Soul of the Coral Coast

Snorkeling with rubber fins,
Fish parade, a laughter spree,
Flippers flapping, doe-eyed grins,
As sea turtles just pass by free.

Coral castles, vibrant and bright,
Homemade maps with wobbly lines,
Adventure lurks, a goofy sight,
While seagulls plot their sneak designs.

Daydreams float on the brisk waves,
Frogs croak jokes just for fun,
The ocean's secrets, how it braves,
Whisper laughter under the sun.

At sun's set, we raise a toast,
With pies made of fruity delight,
To all the wonders we love most,
In this land of pure sunlight.

Canvas of Nature's Palette

Colors splash in wild delight,
Painted fields, what a sight!
Daisies dance, they twist and shout,
While sunflowers wobble, no doubt!

Squirrels race in a fuzzy blur,
Chasing shadows—what a spur!
A parrot squawks a silly joke,
While lazy cows just sit and poke.

Rainbows arch and then they slide,
As turtles wear a humble glide.
Nature's brush strokes, oh so bright,
Make every day a pure delight!

Ballet of the Flickering Fireflies

Twinkling stars in the night sky,
Fireflies frolic, oh so spry!
They do a dance, a jig so bold,
A shining show, a sight to behold!

In a tutu made of dewy grass,
They twirl around with such great class.
Little stars in a twilight ball,
With each flicker, they enthrall!

Crickets chirp a lively beat,
As nature claps with tiny feet.
A nightly laugh, a bright parade,
Where joy is born and never fades!

Life Under an Endless Sky

A canvas wide, a giggle's sound,
Clouds like cotton, all around.
A kite takes flight, a cheeky grin,
As kids run wild, let the fun begin!

Sandy toes and seashells bright,
Splashing waves with pure delight.
Seagulls chat and steal your fries,
While sandcastles meet their demise!

Sunburnt noses, wild sunscreen,
Ice cream drips and laughter's seen.
A sun-drenched world, full of cheer,
Where every day is a souvenir!

Soliloquy of the Evening Tides

The moon reflects on wavy sheen,
While crabs do a dance, unaware of the scene.
Shells whisper tales of tides so bold,
As starfish giggle at stories retold.

Waves run out, then back with a cheer,
"Catch me, I'm here!" they seem to jeer.
A dolphin flips to steal the show,
As gulls swoop down and steal the glow.

The sea breeze sings a lullaby,
While kids chase shadows, oh my, oh my!
Evening settles, with waves that slide,
In the smooth embrace of the playful tide.

The Pulse of the Warm Coastal Wind

A coconut fell, hit me right on the head,
I laughed so hard, I almost got led.
Sand in my shoes, but I'm still on my way,
Chasing beach crabs 'til the end of the day.

Sunburned noses and swimming in strife,
Even the seagulls ponder their life.
Flip-flops are missing, oh what a mess,
But the ocean's a cheerleader, I must confess.

Tanned folks abound, and ice cream in hand,
Dancing with waves, it's all oh-so grand.
Fishermen grumble, they're out of luck,
While beach bums giggle at their crazy pluck.

Tropical breezes, they tickle my toes,
Hula skirts swirling, like nobody knows.
Life's a big party under skies so blue,
With laughter and sunshine, come join the crew!

Lullabies of the Ocean's Breath

The waves sing softly, a gentle croon,
As I nap on the sand like a lazy raccoon.
Seashells tickle my toes as they play,
Even the starfish seem to sway.

A seagull swoops past with a glimmer of glee,
Diving for fries someone dropped by the sea.
I chuckle and munch on a coconut treat,
Waves crashing loudly as life skips a beat.

The crabs throw a dance party, what a surprise,
Chasing their shadows under sunlit skies.
I join in the fun, all flailing and free,
As seaweed wiggles, laughing at me.

With sunblock applied, I'm ready to shine,
Sipping lemonade, oh, this life is divine.
Riding on waves that will never go flat,
Life is a lullaby; imagine that!

Heartbeats in the Tropical Heat

Tropical sun makes me sweat, oh dear,
I wave to the clouds, please bring me some cheer.
Hats flying off like confetti on high,
As I stumble to find shade that feels nigh.

Mango juice drips and it stains my shirt,
But here comes a parrot just ready to flirt.
I laugh as he squawks a peculiar refrain,
In this sunny madness, no room for disdain.

Dancing with chickens, we shimmy and sway,
The rhythm of laughter, come join the ballet.
Flip-flops abandoned, running on sand,
Barefoot and giggling, the world's so unplanned.

With every heartbeat, I feel so alive,
In this place of sunshine, I strive to thrive.
Tropical breezes and friends all around,
Every moment of joy is perfectly found!

Sun-soaked Stories from the Wild

A monkey stole my snack, what a wild show,
He grinned with delight, then made off in a row.
I chased him through trees, full of laughter and fun,
Guess I won't have lunch, but at least I could run.

The dolphins are plotting their swimmy parade,
While I'm stuck sunbathing, what a charade!
Lobsters are laughing, thinking I'm bait,
As I ponder the world and contemplate fate.

A beach party brews, invitations are grand,
I'm a little late due to footprints in sand.
Everyone's dancing, wearing smiles and glee,
As I juggle my drink, what a sight to see!

From bonfire stories to moonlit delights,
Life under the stars, what a series of sights.
So let's toast to the sun, the fun never ends,
In a world where each laugh ties us all as friends!

www.ingramcontent.com/pod-product-compliance
Lightning Source LLC
Chambersburg PA
CBHW072219070526
44585CB00015B/1405